HAL•LEONARD

PIANO PLAY-ALONG

THE 1980s

ISBN 978-1-4234-4958-4

HAL•LEONARD®
CORPORATION
7777 W. BLUEMOUND RD. P.O. BOX 13819 MILWAUKEE, WI 53213

Visit Hal Leonard Online at
www.halleonard.com

ALL NIGHT LONG
(All Night)

Words and Music by
LIONEL RICHIE

Moderate Caribbean feel

8

GOT MY MIND SET ON YOU

Words and Music by
RUDY CLARK

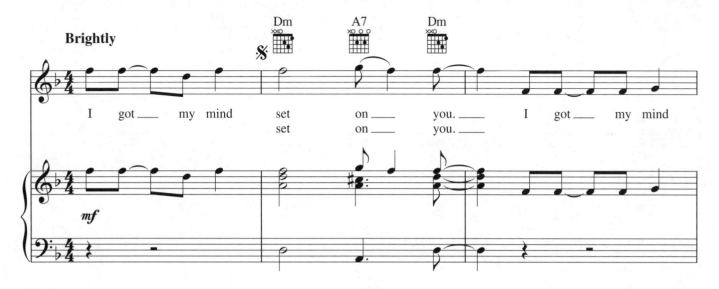

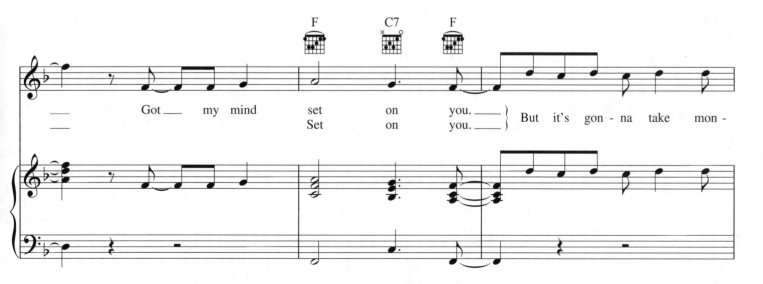

ANOTHER ONE BITES THE DUST

Words and Music by
JOHN DEACON

EVERY LITTLE THING SHE DOES IS MAGIC

Music and Lyrics by
STING

I JUST CALLED TO SAY I LOVE YOU

Words and Music by
STEVIE WONDER

Additional Lyrics

3. No summer's high; no warm July;
   No harvest moon to light one tender August night.
   No autumn breeze; no falling leaves;
   Not even time for birds to fly to southern skies.

4. No Libra sun; no Halloween;
   No giving thanks to all the Christmas joy you bring.
   But what it is, though old so new
   To fill your heart like no three words could ever do.
   Chorus

KOKOMO
from the Motion Picture COCKTAIL

Words and Music by MIKE LOVE,
TERRY MELCHER, JOHN PHILLIPS
and SCOTT McKENZIE

STAND BY ME

Words and Music by JERRY LEIBER,
MIKE STOLLER and BEN E. KING

SAVING ALL MY LOVE FOR YOU

Words by GERRY GOFFIN
Music by MICHAEL MASSER

THE ULTIMATE SONGBOOKS

These great songbook/CD packs come with our standard arrangements for piano and voice with guitar chord frames plus a CD.
The CD includes a full performance of each song, as well as a second track without the piano part so you can play "lead" with the band!

1. Movie Music
Come What May • My Heart Will Go On (Love Theme from *Titanic*) • The Rainbow Connection • and more.
00311072 P/V/G.............$14.95

2. Jazz Ballads
Georgia on My Mind • In a Sentimental Mood • The Nearness of You • The Very Thought of You • When Sunny Gets Blue • and more.
00311073 P/V/G.............$14.95

3. Timeless Pop
Ebony and Ivory • Every Breath You Take • From a Distance • I Write the Songs • In My Room • Let It Be • Oh, Pretty Woman • We've Only Just Begun.
00311074 P/V/G.............$14.95

4. Broadway Classics
Ain't Misbehavin' • Cabaret • If I Were a Bell • Memory • Oklahoma • Some Enchanted Evening • The Sound of Music • You'll Never Walk Alone.
00311075 P/V/G.............$14.95

5. Disney
Beauty and the Beast • Can You Feel the Love Tonight • A Whole New World • You'll Be in My Heart • You've Got a Friend in Me • and more.
00311076 P/V/G.............$14.95

6. Country Standards
Blue Eyes Crying in the Rain • Crazy • King of the Road • Oh, Lonesome Me • Ring of Fire • Tennessee Waltz • You Are My Sunshine • Your Cheatin' Heart.
00311077 P/V/G.............$14.95

7. Love Songs
Can't Help Falling in Love • Here, There and Everywhere • How Deep Is Your Love • Maybe I'm Amazed • You Are So Beautiful • and more.
00311078 P/V/G.............$14.95

8. Classical Themes
Can Can • Habanera • Humoresque • In the Hall of the Mountain King • Minuet in G Major • Symphony No. 5 in C Minor, 1st Movement Excerpt • and more.
00311079 Piano Solo.............$14.95

9. Children's Songs
Do-Re-Mi • It's a Small World • Linus and Lucy • Sesame Street Theme • Sing • Winnie the Pooh • Won't You Be My Neighbor? • Yellow Submarine.
0311080 P/V/G.............$14.95

10. Wedding Classics
Air on the G String • Ave Maria • Bridal Chorus • Canon in D • Jesu, Joy of Man's Desiring • Ode to Joy • Trumpet Voluntary • Wedding March.
00311081 Piano Solo.............$14.95

11. Wedding Favorites
All I Ask of You • Don't Know Much • Endless Love • Grow Old with Me • In My Life • Longer • Wedding Processional • You and I.
00311097 P/V/G.............$14.95

12. Christmas Favorites
Blue Christmas • The Christmas Song • Do You Hear What I Hear • Here Comes Santa Claus • Merry Christmas, Darling • Silver Bells • and more.
00311137 P/V/G.............$15.95

13. Yuletide Favorites
Away in a Manger • Deck the Hall • The First Noel • Go, Tell It on the Mountain • Jingle Bells • Joy to the World • O Little Town of Bethlehem • and more.
00311138 P/V/G.............$14.95

14. Pop Ballads
Have I Told You Lately • I'll Be There for You • Rainy Days and Monday • She's Got a Way • Your Song • and more.
00311145 P/V/G.............$14.95

15. Favorite Standards
Call Me • The Girl from Ipanema • Moon River • My Way • Satin Doll • Smoke Gets in Your Eyes • Strangers in the Night • The Way You Look Tonight.
00311146 P/V/G.............$14.95

16. TV Classics
The Brady Bunch • Green Acres Theme • Happy Days • Johnny's Theme • Love Boat Theme • Mister Ed • The Munsters Theme • Where Everybody Knows Your Name.
00311147 P/V/G.............$14.95

17. Movie Favorites
Back to the Future • Theme from *E.T.* • Footloose • Somewhere in Time • Somewhere Out There • and more.
00311148 P/V/G.............$14.95

18. Jazz Standards
All the Things You Are • Bluesette • Easy Living • I'll Remember April • Isn't It Romantic? • Stella by Starlight • Tangerine • Yesterdays.
00311149 P/V/G.............$14.95

19. Contemporary Hits
Beautiful • Calling All Angels • Don't Know Why • If I Ain't Got You • 100 Years • This Love • A Thousand Miles • You Raise Me Up.
00311162 P/V/G.............$14.95

20. R&B Ballads
After the Love Has Gone • All in Love Is Fair • Hello • I'll Be There • Let's Stay Together • Midnight Train to Georgia • Tell It like It Is • Three Times a Lady.
00311163 P/V/G.............$14.95

21. Big Band
All or Nothing at All • Apple Honey • April in Paris • Cherokee • In the Mood • Opus One • Stardust • Stompin' at the Savoy.
00311164 P/V/G.............$14.95

22. Rock Classics
Against All Odds • Bennie and the Jets • Come Sail Away • Do It Again • Free Bird • Jump • Wanted Dead or Alive • We Are the Champions.
00311165 P/V/G.............$14.95

23. Worship Classics
Awesome God • Lord, Be Glorified • Lord, I Lift Your Name on High • Shine, Jesus, Shine • Step by Step • There Is a Redeemer • and more.
00311166 P/V/G.............$14.95

24. Les Misérables
Bring Him Home • Castle on a Cloud • Empty Chairs at Empty Tables • I Dreamed a Dream • A Little Fall of Rain • On My Own • and more.
00311169 P/V/G.............$14.95

25. The Sound of Music
Climb Ev'ry Mountain • Do-Re-Mi • Edelweiss • Maria • My Favorite Things • Sixteen Going on Seventeen • Something Good • The Sound of Music.
00311175 P/V/G.............$15.99

26. Andrew Lloyd Webber Favorites
All I Ask of You • Amigos Para Siempre • As If We Never Said Goodbye • Everything's Alright • Memory • No Matter What • Tell Me on a Sunday • You Must Love Me.
00311178 P/V/G.............$14.95

27. Andrew Lloyd Webber Greats
Don't Cry for Me Argentina • I Don't Know How to Love Him • The Phantom of the Opera • Whistle down the Wind • With One Look • and more.
00311179 P/V/G.............$14.95

28. Lennon & McCartney
Eleanor Rigby • Hey Jude • The Long and Winding Road • Love Me Do • Lucy in the Sky with Diamonds • Nowhere Man • Strawberry Fields Forever • Yesterday.
00311180 P/V/G.............$14.95

29. The Beach Boys
Barbara Ann • Be True to Your School • California Girls • Fun, Fun, Fun • Help Me Rhonda • I Get Around • Little Deuce Coupe • Wouldn't It Be Nice.
00311181 P/V/G.............$14.95

30. Elton John
Candle in the Wind • Crocodile Rock • Daniel • Goodbye Yellow Brick Road • Guess That's Why They Call It the Blues • Levon • Your Song • and more.
00311182 P/V/G.............$14.95

31. Carpenters
(They Long to Be) Close to You • Only Yesterday • Rainy Days and Mondays • Top of the World • We've Only Just Begun • Yesterday Once More • and more.
00311183 P/V/G.............$14.95

32. Bacharach & David
Alfie • Do You Know the Way to San Jose • The Look of Love • Raindrops Keep Fallin' on My Head • What the World Needs Now Is Love • and more.
00311218 P/V/G.............$14.95

33. Peanuts™
Blue Charlie Brown • Charlie Brown Theme • The Great Pumpkin Waltz • Joe Cool • Linus and Lucy • Oh, Good Grief • Red Baron • You're in Love, Charlie Brown.
00311227 P/V/G.............$14.95

34 Charlie Brown Christmas
Christmas Is Coming • The Christmas Song • Christmas Time Is Here • Linus and Lucy • My Little Drum • O Tannenbaum • Skating • What Child Is This.
00311228 P/V/G.............$15.95

35. Elvis Presley Hits
Blue Suede Shoes • Can't Help Falling in Love • Heartbreak Hotel • Love Me • (Let Me Be Your) Teddy Bear and more.
00311230 P/V/G....................$14.95

36. Elvis Presley Greats
All Shook Up • Don't • Jailhouse Rock • Love Me Tender • Loving You • Return to Sender • Too Much • Wooden Heart.
00311231 P/V/G....................$14.95

37. Contemporary Christian
El Shaddai • Every Season • Here I Am • Jesus Will Still Be There • Let Us Pray • Place in This World • Who Am I • Wisdom.
00311232 P/V/G....................$14.95

38. Duke Ellington Standards
Caravan • I Got It Bad and That Ain't Good • In a Sentimental Mood • Love You Madly • Mood Indigo • Sophisticated Lady • more.
00311233 P/V/G....................$14.95

39. Duke Ellington Classics
Don't Get Around Much Anymore • I Let a Song Go out of My Heart • In a Mellow Tone • Satin Doll • Take the "A" Train • and more.
00311234 P/V/G....................$14.95

40. Showtunes
The Best of Times • Hello, Dolly! • I'll Know • Mame • Summer Nights • Till There Was You • Tomorrow • What I Did for Love.
00311237 P/V/G....................$14.95

41. Rodgers & Hammerstein
Bali Ha'i • Hello, Young Lovers • If I Loved You • It Might as Well Be Spring • Love, Look Away • Oh, What a Beautiful Mornin' • and more.
00311238 P/V/G....................$14.95

42. Irving Berlin
Always • Blue Skies • Change Partners • Cheek to Cheek • Easter Parade • How Deep Is the Ocean (How High Is the Sky) • Puttin' on the Ritz • What'll I Do?
00311239 P/V/G....................$14.95

43. Jerome Kern
Can't Help Lovin' Dat Man • A Fine Romance • I Won't Dance • I'm Old Fashioned • The Last Time I Saw Paris • Ol' Man River • and more.
00311240 P/V/G....................$14.95

44. Frank Sinatra – Popular Hits
Come Fly with Me • Cycles • High Hopes • Love and Marriage • My Way • Strangers in the Night • (Love Is) The Tender Trap • Young at Heart.
00311277 P/V/G....................$14.95

45. Frank Sinatra – Most Requested Songs
From Here to Eternity • I've Got the World on a String • Theme from "New York, New York" • Night and Day • Time After Time • Witchcraft • and more.
00311278 P/V/G....................$14.95

46. Wicked
Dancing Through Life • Defying Gravity • For Good • I Couldn't Be Happier • I'm Not That Girl • Popular • What Is This Feeling? • The Wizard and I.
00311317 P/V/G....................$15.99

47. Rent
I'll Cover You • Light My Candle • One Song Glory • Out Tonight • Rent • Seasons of Love • What You Own • Without You.
00311319 P/V/G....................$14.95

48. Christmas Carols
God Rest Ye Merry, Gentlemen • Hark! the Herald Angels Sing • It Came upon the Midnight Clear • O Holy Night • Silent Night • What Child Is This? • and more.
00311332 P/V/G....................$14.95

49. Holiday Hits
Frosty the Snow Man • Happy Xmas (War Is Over) • I'll Be Home for Christmas • Jingle-Bell Rock • Rudolph the Red-Nosed Reindeer • Santa Claus Is Comin' to Town • and more.
00311333 P/V/G....................$14.95

50. Disney Classics
Some Day My Prince Will Come • When You Wish upon a Star • Whistle While You Work • Who's Afraid of the Big Bad Wolf? • Zip-A-Dee-Doo-Dah • and more.
00311417 P/V/G....................$14.95

51. High School Musical
9 songs, including: Breaking Free • Get'cha Head in the Game • Start of Something New • We're All in This Together • What I've Been Looking For • and more.
00311421 P/V/G....................$19.95

52. Andrew Lloyd Webber Classics
Another Suitcase in Another Hall • Close Every Door • Love Changes Everything • The Perfect Year • Pie Jesu • Wishing You Were Somehow Here Again • and more.
00311422 P/V/G....................$14.95

53. Grease
Beauty School Dropout • Grease • Greased Lightnin' • Hopelessly Devoted to You • Sandy • Summer Nights • You're the One That I Want • and more.
00311450 P/V/G....................$14.95

54. Broadway Favorites
Big Spender • Comedy Tonight • Hello, Young Lovers • I've Grown Accustomed to Her Face • Just in Time • Make Someone Happy • My Ship • People.
00311451 P/V/G....................$14.95

55. The 1940s
Come Rain or Come Shine • It Could Happen to You • Moonlight in Vermont • A Nightingale Sang in Berkeley Square • Route 66 • Sentimental Journey • and more.
00311453 P/V/G....................$14.95

56. The 1950s
Blueberry Hill • Dream Lover • Fever • The Great Pretender • Kansas City • Memories Are Made of This • My Prayer • Put Your Head on My Shoulder.
00311459 P/V/G....................$14.95

57. The 1960s
Beyond the Sea • Blue Velvet • California Dreamin' • Downtown • For Once in My Life • Let's Hang On • (Sittin' On) The Dock of the Bay • The Twist.
00311460 P/V/G....................$14.99

58. The 1970s
Dust in the Wind • Everything Is Beautiful • How Can You Mend a Broken Heart • I Feel the Earth Move • If • Joy to the World • My Eyes Adored You • You've Got a Friend.
00311461 P/V/G....................$14.99

61. Billy Joel Favorites
And So It Goes • Baby Grand • It's Still Rock and Roll to Me • Leave a Tender Moment Alone • Piano Man • She's Always a Woman • Uptown Girl • You May Be Right.
00311464 P/V/G....................$14.95

62. Billy Joel Hits
The Entertainer • Honesty • Just the Way You Are • The Longest Time • Lullabye (Goodnight, My Angel) • My Life • New York State of Mind • She's Got a Way.
00311465 P/V/G....................$14.95

63. High School Musical 2
All for One • Everyday • Fabulous • Gotta Go My Own Way • I Don't Dance • What Time Is It • Work This Out • You Are the Music in Me.
00311470 P/V/G....................$19.95

64. God Bless America
America • America, the Beautiful • Anchors Aweigh • Battle Hymn of the Republic • God Bless America • This Is My Country • This Land Is Your Land • and more.
00311489 P/V/G....................$14.95

65. Casting Crowns
Does Anybody Hear Her • East to West • Here I Go Again • Praise You in This Storm • Somewhere in the Middle • Voice of Truth • While You Were Sleeping • Who Am I.
00311494 P/V/G....................$14.95

66. Hannah Montana
I Got Nerve • Just like You • Life's What You Make It • Nobody's Perfect • Old Blue Jeans • Pumpin' up the Party • Rock Star • We Got the Party.
00311772 P/V/G....................$19.95

67. Broadway Gems
Getting to Know You • I Could Have Danced All Night • If I Were a Rich Man • It's a Lovely Day Today • September Song • The Song Is You • and more.
00311803 P/V/G....................$14.99

68. Lennon & McCartney Favorites
All My Loving • The Fool on the Hill • A Hard Day's Night • Here, There and Everywhere • I Saw Her Standing There • Yellow Submarine • and more.
00311804 P/V/G....................$14.95

69. Pirates of the Caribbean
All for One • Everyday • Fabulous • Gotta Go My Own Way • I Don't Dance • What Time Is It • Work This Out • You Are the Music in Me.
00311807 P/V/G....................$14.95

70. "Tomorrow," "Put on a Happy Face," And Other Charles Strouse Hits
Born Too Late • A Lot of Livin' to Do • Night Song • Once upon a Time • Put on a Happy Face • Those Were the Days • Tomorrow • You've Got Possibilities.
00311821 P/V/G....................$14.99

71. Rock Band
Black Hole Sun • Don't Fear the Reaper • Learn to Fly • Paranoid • Say It Ain't So • Suffragette City • Wanted Dead or Alive • Won't Get Fooled Again.
00311822 P/V/G....................$14.99

72. High School Musical 3
Can I Have This Dance • High School Musical • I Want It All • A Night to Remember • Now or Never • Right Here Right Now • Scream • Walk Away.
00311826 P/V/G....................$19.99

73. Mamma Mia! – The Movie
Dancing Queen • Gimme! Gimme! Gimme! (A Man After Midnight) • Honey, Honey • Lay All Your Love on Me • Mamma Mia • SOS • Take a Chance on Me • The Winner Takes It All.
00311831 P/V/G....................$14.99

THE DECADE SERIES

The Decade Series explores the music of the 1890s to the 1990s through each era's major events and personalities. Each volume features text and photos and over 40 of the decade's top songs, showing how music has acted as a mirror or a catalyst for current events and trends. All books are arranged for piano, voice and guitar.

Songs of the 1890s
55 songs: Hello! Ma Baby • Maple Leaf Rag • My Wild Irish Rose • The Sidewalks of New York • Stars and Stripes Forever • When You Were Sweet Sixteen • and more.
00311655 ....$12.95

Songs of the 1900s (1900-1909)
57 favorites: By the Light of the Silvery Moon • Give My Regards to Broadway • Glow Worm • Meet Me in St. Louis • Take Me Out to the Ball Game • and more.
00311656 ....$12.95

Songs of the 1910s
57 classics: After You've Gone • Danny Boy • Let Me Call You Sweetheart • My Melancholy Baby • Oh, You Beautiful Doll • When Irish Eyes Are Smiling • and more.
00311657 ....$12.95

Songs of the '20s
59 songs: Ain't Misbehavin' • April Showers • Baby Face • California Here I Come • Five Foot Two, Eyes of Blue • Manhattan • The Varsity Drag • Who's Sorry Now • more.
00361122 ....$15.95

Songs of the '30s
62 standards: All of Me • In the Mood • The Lady Is a Tramp • Love Letters in the Sand • My Funny Valentine • Smoke Gets in Your Eyes • What a Diff'rence a Day Made • more.
00361123 ....$15.95

Songs of the '40s
62 classics: God Bless the Child • How High the Moon • The Last Time I Saw Paris • A Nightingale Sang in Berkeley Square • Swinging On a Star • Tuxedo Junction • more.
00361124 ....$17.95

Songs of the '50s - 2nd Edition
62 songs: Blue Suede Shoes • Blue Velvet • Here's That Rainy Day • Love Me Tender • Misty • Rock Around the Clock • Satin Doll • Tammy • Young at Heart • and more.
00361125 ....$16.95

Songs of the '60s - 2nd Edition
62 tunes: By the Time I Get to Phoenix • California Dreamin' • Can't Help Falling in Love • Happy Together • I Want to Hold Your Hand • Strangers in the Night • and more.
00361126 ....$16.95

Songs of the '70s
More than 45 songs: Feelings • How Deep Is Your Love • Imagine • Let It Be • Me and Bobby McGee • Piano Man • Send in the Clowns • You Don't Bring Me Flowers • more.
00361127 ....$16.95

Songs of the '80s
Over 40 hits: Candle in the Wind • Ebony and Ivory • Every Breath You Take • Flashdance...What a Feeling • Islands in the Stream • What's Love Got to Do with It • and more.
00490275 ....$16.95

Songs of the '90s
39 great songs: Achy Breaky Heart • Beautiful in My Eyes • Friends in Low Places • Here and Now • Losing My Religion • Save the Best for Last • Tears in Heaven • and more.
00310151 ....$16.95

Songs of the 2000s
35 tunes: Beautiful • Breakaway • Complicated • Don't Know Why • The Space Between • Underneath It All • White Flag • You Raise Me Up • and more.
00311340 ....$16.95

More Songs of the '20s
Over 50 songs: Ain't We Got Fun? • Fascinating Rhythm • Malagueña • Nobody Knows You When You're Down and Out • Someone to Watch Over Me • and more.
00311647 ....$15.99

More Songs of the '30s - 2nd Edition
Over 50 favorites: All the Things You Are • A Fine Romance • In a Sentimental Mood • Stompin' at the Savoy • Stormy Weather • Thanks for the Memory • and more.
00311648 ....$15.99

More Songs of the '40s
60 songs: Bali Ha'i • Be Careful, It's My Heart • San Antonio Rose • Some Enchanted Evening • Too Darn Hot • and more.
00311649 ....$15.95

More Songs of the '50s - 2nd Edition
Over 50 songs: Charlie Brown • Hey, Good Lookin' • Hound Dog • Mona Lisa • (Let Me Be Your) Teddy Bear • That's Amoré • and more.
00311650 ....$15.95

More Songs of the '60s - 2nd Edition
Over 60 songs: Alfie • Born to Be Wild • Moon River • Raindrops Keep Fallin' On My Head • Sweet Caroline • What the World Needs Now • Wooly Bully • and more.
00311651 ....$15.95

More Songs of the '70s
Over 50 songs: Afternoon Delight • All By Myself • American Pie • Happy Days • She Believes in Me • She's Always a Woman • Wishing You Were Here • and more.
00311652 ....$15.95

More Songs of the '80s
43 songs: Addicted to Love • Footloose • Girls Just Want to Have Fun • The Heat Is On • Karma Chameleon • Take My Breath Away • and more.
00311653 ....$15.95

More Songs of the '90s
Over 30 hits: Blue • Butterfly Kisses • Change the World • Give Me One Reason • I Don't Want to Wait • My Father's Eyes • My Heart Will Go On • more.
00310430 ....$15.95

Even More Songs of the '40s
Over 50 classics: Easy Street • It Could Happen to You • Sioux City Sue • Steppin' Out with My Baby • and more.
00311194 ....$14.95

Even More Songs of the '50s - 2nd Edition
Over 60 great songs: Dream Lover • Great Balls of Fire • La Bamba • Love and Marriage • Wake Up Little Susie • more.
00310986 ....$14.95

Even More Songs of the '60s
59 super hits: Daydream Believer • Good Vibrations • My Girl • Respect • Twist and Shout • Yesterday • and more.
00310987 ....$14.95

Even More Songs of the '70s
51 top songs: I Honestly Love You • I'll Be There • Joy to the World • Time in a Bottle • Y.M.C.A. • and more.
00310988 ....$14.95

Even More Songs of the '80s
39 hits: Chariots of Fire • Jack and Diane • Lady in Red • Missing You • Thriller • Walk Like an Egyptian • more.
00311031 ....$14.95

Still More Songs of the '30s - 2nd Edition
Over 50 songs: April in Paris • Heat Wave • It Don't Mean a Thing (If It Ain't Got That Swing) • and more.
00310027 ....$15.95

Still More Songs of the '40s
Over 50 favorites: Don't Get Around Much Anymore • If I Loved You • Sentimental Journey • and more.
00310028 ....$15.95

Still More Songs of the '50s - 2nd Edition
Over 50 classics: Autumn Leaves • Chantilly Lace • If I Were a Bell • Luck Be a Lady • Venus • and more.
00310029 ....$15.95

Still More Songs of the '60s
Over 50 songs: Duke of Earl • I'm Henry VIII, I Am • Leader of the Pack • What a Wonderful World • and more.
00311680 ....$15.95

Still More Songs of the '70s
54 hits: Cat's in the Cradle • Nadia's Theme • The Way We Were • You've Got a Friend • and more.
00311683 ....$15.95

Still More Songs of the '80s
40 songs: All I Need • Jessie's Girl • Sweet Dreams (Are Made of This) • Up Where We Belong • and more.
00310321 ....$15.95

Still More Songs of the '90s
40 hits: Fields of Gold • From a Distance • Jump Jive An' Wail • Kiss Me • Mambo No. 5 • and more.
00310575 ....$15.95

FOR MORE INFORMATION,
SEE YOUR LOCAL MUSIC DEALER,
OR WRITE TO:

HAL•LEONARD® CORPORATION
7777 W. BLUEMOUND RD. P.O. BOX 13819
MILWAUKEE, WISCONSIN 53213

Prices, contents, and availability
subject to change without notice
Complete contents listings available online at
www.halleonard.com.